Plan ahead boomers,
we are entering the end of fall in our lives.

BOOMER BEWARE!

THE CLOCK IS TICKING DOWN

LOOKING BACK ON
7 DECADES.

MICHAEL DALE MOSLEY

Boomers Beware! The Clock is Ticking Down

by Michael Dale Mosley

TABLE OF CONTENTS

DEDICATION 4

ABOUT THE AUTHOR 5

INTRODUCTION 7

CHAPTER 1 The First 10 Years 1945 to 1955 12

CHAPTER 2 1955 to 1965 15

CHAPTER 3 1965 to 1975 18

CHAPTER 4 1975 to 1985 21

CHAPTER 5 1985 to 1995 24

CHAPTER 6 1995 to 2005 27

CHAPTER 7 2005 to 2015 31

CHAPTER 8 2015 to 2025 35

SOURCES 45

DEDICATION

This book is dedicated to my brother, Ted Mosley. Like me, he is a Baby Boomer, having been born in 1946. He has been a mentor to me for 77 years. Ted holds a master's degree, and he loves our National Parks, especially Yellowstone and Yosemite.

ABOUT THE AUTHOR

The Author of this book is a 77-year-old Baby Boomer. Michael Mosley has authored two other books.   In the words of Mr. Mosley…" I am a not a great writer, but I have a lot of great stories to tell." This is his 3rd book.

Mosley holds a BS in Education and a MA in School Counseling/Health. Mr. Mosley was a college Professor of Health and Wellness for 6 years, in Georgia. He also taught in the Governor's Honors Program at Valdosta State.   The Author had a 37-year career in Education, K through University. He is an award-winning Educator and is a member of Who's Who in American Education. In February of 2025, the Governor of Kentucky commissioned him, "A Kentucky Colonel," for his contributions to the Commonwealth of Kentucky. Mosley is fully retired and has traveled to 41 countries and 44 states, two principalities, and four provinces. He is a father and grandfather and serves on his local HOA. He was educated in Kentucky. (BS at EKU MA at WKU).

London High School – London, Kentucky

INTRODUCTION

This book will be divided into 8 parts, with each representing 10 years. In each decade, we will look back on what Baby Boomers were doing at that time in history.

Adobe Express Photo

1. **The hospitals fill up with new babies.** (1945–1955)
   The Baby Boom begins and nurseries overflow across America.

2. **New schools must be built for all these bratty new kids.** (1955–1965)
   Suburbs expand, and so do school districts.

3. **Off to Vietnam for so many Boomers, as the classes of '65–'67 get's drafted.** (1965–1975)
   Waterloo for 58,400. War defines a generation.

4. **College and the World of Work.** (1975–1985)
   Boomers settle into careers, marriage, and suburban life.

5. **Starting a family, building a house, new jobs... Oh no, middle age knocks on the door.** (1985–1995)

6. **Getting ahead in the rat race. Changing jobs. Changing spouses. Moving. Chasing the American Dream.** (1995–2005)
   Our parents begin to leave our world.

7. **Grandchildren. Receding hairlines. The beginning of health issues. Sex is no longer a driving force.** (2005–2015)
   Retirement looms. A longtime partner or spouse dies. The question arises: *Can I live alone?*

8. **The End of Years – A look back and a look forward.** (2015–2025)
   Reflection. Acceptance. Gratitude. Mortality.

We will look at recent trends and look at what is to come. And we will ask that painful question: are we starting to die off?

Now comes the time to prepare the Will. Pre-planning at the funeral home. The medicine cabinet looks like a small pharmacy. Can I live on this measly Social Security check? Precious Lord, take my hand… Did you know?

THE COMMONLY ACCEPTED NOTIONS ABOUT THE BOOMERS

Let's look at these people called "Baby Boomers." They are post-war babies, for the most part. But don't be fooled by those who claim the Boomer era runs all the way to 1964. People born in 1946 and people born in 1964 are not birds of a feather. The real baby boom starts in 1945 as the two wars ended. The war in Europe ended in the spring of '45, and the Japanese surrendered nearly six months later. It was after the war ended in Japan that the boys came home.

There are approximately 77 million Boomers. Although many are in their 70s now, some continue to work and make a very positive contribution to society.

The Boomer generation got "sucker punched" when the Information Age arrived. But don't be fooled by this, as they catch on quickly and are hitting their stride late in life. Boomers are very aware of the environment and what is taking place around them. Remember, they were born into a world that was not polluted, or overpopulated, and there were very few animals on the endangered species list.

Boomers have CASH! That's right, they may be old and worn out from 40 years of work, but they knew the value of a dollar. On the other hand, you can walk into many Wendy's or McDonald's and see 72-year-old women still working.

Boomers tend to stick to "traditional brands." Campbell's soup, Tide washing detergent, and Bud Light beer can still be found in their homes. It's a shame Bud Walton did not live to see his stores become a shrine to Boomers. But there are limits to what Boomers would put up with in the marketplace. Many Boomers refused to buy Ford, Chevy, Buick, and Oldsmobile products when they literally fell apart within months. They switched to Nissan, Hyundai, and Honda products and some of us NEVER WENT BACK.

Boomers are often called happy-go-lucky people. But there are equally as many "Type A Boomers" who mow their lawn weekly, paint the house every seven years, and are first in line to vote come election day. And don't even think of sitting in their pew at church. A hard stare from a Boomer is far more powerful than words.

The Boomer generation loves big events: the World Series, Election Day, Decoration Day, Homecoming, the Final Four and when Christmas rolls around, they are the first to put up a tree. You'll find Christmas ornaments that date back 40 years, and if you have smart remarks about them, you would do well to keep them to yourself.

Parents of the Boomers were prone to regular church attendance, but they somehow failed to inspire "regular" church attendance in their children. The majority of Boomers are Christian (54%) and less than 6% are atheist.

Boomers have moved around during their seven decades. They doubled the population of Georgia in 30 years. But their first choices are California, New Hampshire, Vermont, and the Sun Belt. Places they like the most are: Palm Coast, Florida; Cape Coral, Florida; Scottsdale, Arizona; and Sunrise, Florida.

Because their parents had funerals, the Boomer generation would like to continue that tradition—but the funeral industry in America has priced itself out of business. Boomers are evenly split between the traditional funeral and cremation.

CHAPTER 1
The First 10 Years 1945 to 1955

Before we look at the early years of the Boomers, it's important to glance back and look at what was happening just prior to the birth of the Boomers.

The 1930s was a gloomy and long decade. They were rocked by the Great Depression, and back then most Americans did NOT live in big cities. They were much more rural and very poor. In fact, poverty embraced the entire country. And just when things could not get worse, the Dust Bowl hit many of the Plains states. There was a huge increase in CRIME and crime rates. The problems were mostly blamed on Herbert Hoover. America began to sink into isolation. 9,000 banks closed their doors for good. Roosevelt was elected to mend the country's woes. Congress quickly passed many of his programs and projects.

Americans were shocked when, in 1939, Germany and the Nazi Party began what would be a long and deadly war that would last five years. America did its best to stay out of the war but was attacked on Dec. 7th, 1941. Young and middle-aged men went off to war, and they would not come home for years. Millions around the world lost their lives in the war. In 1945, both the Japanese and Germans surrendered, and the AMERICAN SOLDIERS CAME HOME.

When Johnny came marching home, he wasted no time in finding a bride, started building a little love nest… and got busy in the bedroom. In 9 months, the babies arrived, and doctors went from delivering one baby a month to FIVE in one day. So now we have the birth of the Boomers. Born into a changing world; new houses went up, young Americans bought cars, radios, and refrigerators. Banks boomed as the veterans had a few coins, and they could not wait to buy property and start a new life. Happy days are here again.

Baby Boomers soon had several brothers and sisters, and in the early 1950s, they headed off to school. (Kindergarten did not exist in most of the South.) Many will tell you that they attended two-room schools that had a pot-belly stove, and many schools had outhouses. Many Boomers in the South remember taking lunch to school (and it consisted of jelly and crackers, and peanut butter sandwiches). Many Boomers coined the phrase, "We were poor, but we did not know it." Today's youth have no clue what after-school "chores" are.
But Boomers sure do, and some tell of taking off their school clothes before work began. This was how the great work ethic in Boomers began. By the mid-50s, Boomer families bought televisions and began summer trips to our State and National Parks.

The Korean War did not have the devastating effects on American life as WWII. Boomers have memories of an uncle or two who did fight in this war.
Since I was born in 1948, I am a true Boomer. Some of my

memories of the first ten years are: uncles who were still in uniform, Christmas with gifts, the two-room schools, 4-H Club, running around the school playground yelling "I Like IKE," and older boys at school getting a paddling. I remember snowy long winters, having many first cousins, skating on the frozen pond, and climbing to the top of the barn to look at bird eggs. Climbing to the top of June apple trees for a sweet and ripe apple was a daily ritual. Hoeing weeds in the garden and tobacco patch was a part of life. Chores, and more chores. I remember having an afternoon snack with a red ripe tomato in one hand and a saltshaker in the other.

By 1955, many women had joined the workforce. This was not the JUNE CLEAVER era. *Leave it to Beaver* and *Father Knows Best* were not true depictions of real life in America. But it did give us hope for the future.

CHAPTER 2
1955 to 1965

The 1st School in America was in St. Augustine, Florida.

My high school classmates.

Many Boomers look back on this decade as the "School Years." High school graduations doubled in size. It was a busy decade around the world. In this span of time, the Suez Canal was built. The Eisenhower Interstate System was started. Little did we know that it would NEVER end. There was a Hungarian Revolution. And we listened to Elvis Presley sing "Heartbreak Hotel" on the radio.

Suburbs began to pop up around big cities. The middle class was born, and hard-working Boomers worked their way into it.

Sputnik caught Americans off guard. Thanks to John F. Kennedy, we soon caught up to the Russians. The ONE event in a Boomer's life that they have never forgotten… is the assassination of President Kennedy. Every Boomer can tell you exactly where they were on that sad day. The world stood still for three days.

The standard of living in the U.S. rose during this decade. People worked hard and moved up. More Boomers went to college than ever before. Grocery stores opened, with up to 10 aisles of food to choose from. Teenagers collected "records." Kids played with hula hoops. Clothing styles changed drastically, as did cars, movies, and Lord knows those Beatles changed music forever.

More Americans were moving to large cities. Boomers did not know, but around the corner was another dark and dreary war: Vietnam. Boomers would bear the brunt of this war.

Some 58,400 Americans (mostly Boomers) were drafted and never came home. Many came home to a thankless homeland. They came home with missing limbs, too.

The American people, for the first time in history, were split on this issue. The Vietnam War divided us. The evening news was filled with video of Boomers being flown home to Delaware in flag-draped caskets.

Not all Boomers served. Donald J. Trump (born in 1946) claimed he suffered from bone spurs and did not serve.

CHAPTER 3
1965 to 1975

In the late '60s, Boomers were around 19 years old. This decade saw the country go through economic prosperity and technological growth. Boomers have lived much of their lives during the COLD WAR. To speak of Russia was like speaking of the Devil himself. Remember, this generation remembers hiding under their school chairs for protection from an atomic blast. Shootings did take place in their lives, and they vividly remember the Robert Kennedy and Dr. Martin Luther King shootings.

Civil Rights bills were passed to ensure that all people (Black and Brown) would be given an equal opportunity to enjoy the new prosperity. The Hippie Generation was born… and yes, many Boomers hopped on board. Woodstock was their masterpiece. Americans watched on TV as the Wood - stockers promoted love, peace, and happiness. Conservative Americans called them potheads and scoffed at the headbands, beads, bell-bottoms, and open sex.

The Feminist Movement took hold, and suddenly, Women's Rights took center stage. The birth control pill was in most young ladies' medicine cabinets or well-hidden in their purse. Boomers embraced these new trends as the new way of life. "Go with the flow…" became common. Power to the People! Americans relaxed their way of life.

By now, Nixon had ended the war and adopted the new All-Volunteer Army. America put a man on the moon, and we were all proud.
Boomers began graduating college in record numbers. Many were the first in their family to ever attend and graduate. Colleges doubled in size. State teachers' colleges quickly changed their name to "university." The National Defense Student Loan helped Appalachian students stay in school and complete their degrees. Boomers were beginning to marry and move out of their parents' house.

By 1970, some Boomers had started families—not large families like their parents had. Boomers were smart to use their VA benefits to pay for college and that first home loan.

Because Boomers make up one-third of all voters, their vote is highly sought after. Trying to figure out how they vote is a bit puzzling, as they have voted both the liberal and conservative ballot. They pay close attention to Social Security, Medicare, tax rates, and inflation. Over the decades, it is safe to say they vote center-right. Seventy-seven percent of all Boomers do show up and vote.

Because of their strong work ethic, Boomers entered the world of work and quickly moved up the ladder. They brought many skills to the workplace.

CHAPTER 4
1975 to 1985

The era of discontent arrives. The Boomers show discontent with traditional institutions. They lose faith that Social Security will be available in their retirement years. While some Boomers were adding on degrees and moving up the managerial ladder, others dropped out of many traditional parts of life.

The Carter years brought a downturn in the economy, although most Boomers voted for the peanut farmer, who was laid to rest just recently after 99 years of life.

Community colleges sprang up everywhere. Boomers grew their hair long and made fun of Generation X, which they referred to as Generation BUST.

In 1980, Boomers were in their early thirties, and while some stayed put and raised families, others got divorces, moved across the country, and started new jobs with new spouses. Boomers questioned everything during this decade. Why is my 401(k) shrinking? Could the government be trusted? Could banks be trusted? Could contractors be trusted? And when Three Mile Island melted down... could nuclear energy be trusted anymore? Why could they not find a cure for this new disease called AIDS?

Boomers looked in crazy places for solutions, and because of that kind of thinking: Jim Jones formed a cult that eventually ended in the death of 144 followers who drank the Kool-Aid. For some, it was the best of times; for others… the worst of times.

By now, Boomers had lost all four grandparents and many uncles and aunts. In the middle of your life, you begin to ask that fateful question: How long will I live? It does occupy your thoughts at this age. We tend to push it to the back of our minds, thinking we have many years to go.

On a positive note, some Boomers were busy running the local Little League. They got active in the PTA, helped with Boys and Girls Clubs, and became loyal college fans, as well as fans of the NBA, NCAA, MLB, and especially NASCAR.

This generation filled up stadiums to follow their favorite teams. They followed college football and basketball religiously. Stadiums had to be expanded… even at Ohio State, Alabama, and Wisconsin. Even schools that had no success in the past 30 years (Kentucky football) saw the need to expand stadiums and arenas. Boomers love sports. Still do. The CBS Selection Show to pick the 68 teams to play in the BB Classic has become one of the most-watched events on television.

Below is a good example of growth and expansion:

New conferences have begun to pop up. Before long, Boomers would not have to cross the country to see their team. The Georgia Southern, Western Kentucky, UTSA, Toledo, and Murray States… joined 1-A sports and changed college sports for the better.

To give you an example of how fervent we were: I, along with a good buddy, got up on a Saturday morning and hopped on a plane from Atlanta to Dallas to watch KENTUCKY play VaTech in the NCAA Tournament at Reunion Arena. We cheered the Cats on to victory and then took a cab back to the airport and arrived back in Atlanta by 6 p.m. that same day.

Boomers do crazy things.

CHAPTER 5
1985 to 1995

Oh Lordy! The Boomers hit 40. They have entered the phase of life where people reflect on their accomplishments (or not) and look to the future for what they might be. Many Boomers are well established in their careers. The majority are married, and many are living a middle-class lifestyle. But working full-time jobs and raising a family is not an easy task.

They question things. Did I enter the right profession? Is our marriage going to last? Could I have done better? These thoughts run through the minds of all middle-aged people.

It's also during this decade that America must face up to the fact that far too many are OBESE.

Did some of us get "Middle Aged Crazy"? Oh, hell yes!

Boomers start to open up IRAs, CDs, annuities, and look at long-range plans. Their older children are graduating high school. Did we save enough for college? Are they attending the right schools?

Boomers are constantly hearing about another generation that did GREAT things, and society is pouring out great honors on them. They are the GREATEST GENERATION, and they are called that, for the most part, because they fought in and won World War II. Boomers fought in Viet Nam and were shunned upon their return home not to mention that many would be plagued by Agent Orange for the rest of their lives.

Basically, Americans were sick of WAR!

Because the Boomer Generation is by far the LARGEST generation of people living on the planet, they have a history of "overcrowding" every aspect of life (schools, churches, hospitals, workplaces). They impact everything.

At age 40, some of them are now doctors, lawyers, professors, mayors, governors, and senators. Bill Clinton becomes one of the first Boomers to reach the White House. Boomers felt that they could relate to the man from Hope, Arkansas.

However, there are over six different pictures of Bill Clinton boarding Jeffrey Epstein's private jet to the U.S. Virgin Islands for sex with teenagers.
(Source: Netflix *Epstein – Filthy Rich*, 3-hour documentary, after Epstein hanged himself in jail.)

You be the judge.

The Mall

Money corrupts completely. Two others who walk free, but pictures do not lie: Donald Trump and Prince Andrew.

Other things that were going on in this decade include: the Valdez oil spill, Game Boy released by Nintendo, and Taylor Swift was born. Eastern European countries demanded freedom from Russia and got it. The European Union is established, and *The Oprah Winfrey Show* becomes America's favorite.

FACT: Did you know that the Baby Boomer Generation is the most vaccinated generation on the planet? No polio in this group.

CHAPTER 6
1995 to 2005

Baby Boomers, by the thousands (approx. 30,000), volunteered to help host the 1996 Olympic Games in Atlanta. The 26th Olympiad was the first to be held in the American South **Atlanta**. It was a whopping success. 193 countries sent athletes, and the opening ceremonies, which I participated in, had a crowd of 85,000 at Olympic Stadium, and millions watched from around the world on TV.

By 1996, we Boomers who were born in 1948 were 48 years old. Some say we were risk-takers. We began to put a high priority on our possessions: cars, condos, even our Tommy Hilfiger clothes.

Many Boomers began to show great disdain for "the ME generation." This decade included the likes of *Forrest Gump*, *Pulp Fiction*, *Cheers*, *The Golden Girls*, and *SNL*. We said goodbye to one of the longest-running shows, *The Tonight Show* with Johnny Carson.

There is a lot of confusion about other generations that ran parallel to the Boomers, like Generation X, Millennials, even the Silent Generation but no generation topped the Boomers.

None of us saw it coming, but the one event that would change the world for decades happened on September 11th, 2001... the terrorist attack on the Twin Towers in NYC. This is another event that everybody living today can say remember exactly where they were on that horrific day.

Nobody *but nobody* had been brave enough to attack the American homeland. For this… terrorists are paying with their lives, even to this day. It took years to find the leader of Iraq, Saddam Hussein, and even more time to hunt down and kill Osama Bin Laden. But find him, we did… and shot him right between the eyes. **Way to go, SEAL Team 6.**

The War on Terrorism led us to fight in Afghanistan for over a decade. We paid dearly for this long war. The flights bringing the dead soldiers home to Delaware reminded us of the Vietnam War.

By 2003, the Boomers made up 82% of the American workforce. In their 50s now… Boomers started looking forward to their retirement years.

A shocking fact about the Boomers is that they had yet another divorce. This is called "Gray Divorce" … getting a divorce after you are 50 years old. It happened—and it happened often. Some Boomers were now marrying for the third time. Just as they overloaded every aspect of life, so did they overload the divorce courts.

On a more positive note, Boomers broke all the records when it came to travel. Boomers loved to travel, and the travel industry was more than willing to plan, book, and escort them to every corner of the globe.

I am proud to say I spent 25 years traveling every summer to all parts of the world. There are no countries in Europe that I did not travel to. I walked on the Great Wall of China, walked around the Pyramids of Egypt, and fell in love with the Sydney Opera House.

Check out my travel book, *Memoirs of a World Traveler*, **on Amazon.com**.

CHAPTER 7
2005 to 2015

Because old age comes upon you slowly, you do your best to deny it, ignore it, and cover it up. Boomers were beginning to retire, yet other Boomers were still working part-time. They found themselves taking care of their elderly parents and financially helping their own children. My daughter's A/C went out last year, and I sent her $500 to help.

Half of the Boomers began saying, "I can't afford to retire." This was also the era of volunteering. I spent two years as a volunteer at the New Georgia Aquarium and loved every minute of it. By the end of the second year, I could name 60% of all the creatures living there.

Boomers who had smoked now began to pay the price. COPD, lung cancer, and heart attacks began to take a toll on them. But as a generation, the number one malady was **hypertension** (high blood pressure) another silent killer. It was quite common to see **Losartan** in the medicine cabinet, and **Zolpidem** to aid with a new problem: sleep issues.

Some Boomers began to look at living in other parts of the country to pay lower taxes. Once again, the Boomers and their big numbers made Florida an overcrowded state with 23 million people and they are still coming in 2025. *The Villages* started building 50 years ago and have never stopped. Swamplands were drained to build hospitals and homes in the Orlando area.

The Apple iPhone came out, and everybody just had to have one. By now, every home had a computer, and many had an iPad to do quick searches no matter where they were.

Obama was elected, proving once and for all, America was not a racial country. We were proud of him and all the things he did. He brought dignity and honesty to the White House. NASA sent a rover to Mars. But a great recession was looming.

The 2008 financial calamity was over by 2015. Americans would never trust Wall Street again, nor insurance conglomerates.

Boston

Elsewhere: The massive Bird Nest Stadium was built in Beijing as the 2008 Olympics were hosted by the Chinese. The opening ceremonies were spectacular.

Marijuana began to show up on voting initiatives, and for the most part, Boomers voted to make its sale legal with lots of strings attached. Northern California was ahead of the game. I took a West Coast tour that started in San Diego and ended in Seattle.

When our tour bus arrived in the small towns of Northern California, the tour director advised us **not** to talk to people in the breakfast restaurants! You see, those who were growing Mary Jane on the hillsides were paranoid that anyone in the restaurant just might be a federal agent. The federal government has never relaxed their laws on marijuana.

I looked forward to seeing the Redwoods and crossing over into Coos Bay, Oregon. In Oregon and Washington, we saw of all things cranberry bogs. Who knew?

I loved Portland, Oregon, and the Rose Garden on the Hill… and the Boomer generation had long ago claimed this city as one of their favorites.

Around the world, this was happening:
A massive earthquake rocked Haiti.

In the Middle East, Arab Spring sent a message that people in that part of the world wanted more civil rights, equality, and justice.

Don't Ask, Don't Tell opened the doors for gay men to serve in the American military.

A massive tsunami killed hundreds in Japan and it was all caught on camera.

Prince William (soon to be the King of England) married Kate, and in no time, an heir to the throne arrived.

CHAPTER 8
2015 to 2025

(THE LAST CHAPTER, LITERALLY)

The "COVID-19 Pandemic"

The COVID-19 pandemic, which killed millions—including my dear sister, **Connie Mosley Martin (1945–2022)**—completely overwhelms anything else that happened during the past decade. Nothing came close to that.

Boomers are now drawing their Social Security checks, and some have become **civically involved**. They have grandchildren in college and help some. Others say they've maxed out their credit cards.

Health systems have sprung up to aid Boomers: Independent Living, VA Clinics and Hospitals, and last but not least Assisted Living and Hospice Care. Researchers say it now takes $44,000 a year to care for a Boomer, $12,000 a year for medications, and as much as $16,000 a year in insurance premiums.

Donald Trump pandered to the lowest levels of society and was elected President.
"An uneducated electorate is the enemy of democracy."

His second presidency turned into a **Revenge Presidency**, and he survived an attempt on his life. Millions marched against both Trump and Musk, and a cabinet that well, you know *"Bring in the Clowns."* Americans are not divided… Trump followers are starting to wake up to reality. They sense that he is leading them down a very slippery slope.

By 2025, there are 1.4 million Boomers already living in nursing centers. That number will continue to grow.
Fox News was fined **$747 million** for misinformation and propaganda. Russia was caught meddling in our elections.

Life expectancy had reached 77 years in the U.S., but thanks to a pandemic and the opioid epidemic, it began sliding downward. Thousands in every state died of fentanyl overdoses. Around the world, our allies ask,
"Why do Americans take so many drugs?"
In my travels to 41 countries, I asked people, *"What's your opinion of Americans?"*
Their most frequent answers?

- ☒ "Your people are fat."

- ☒ "Your people aren't smart."

- ☒ "Your people know almost no geography."
  And then they'd add: *"Well, you asked!"*

Artificial Intelligence (AI) was born, and the likes of Elon Musk and Mark Zuckerberg warn us of its danger.

The environment is now on everyone's mind.
Record-setting hurricanes Irma, Hermine, and Milton hit the

U.S. and travel all the way to Asheville, NC, killing hundreds. Fires blanketed North America, even Greenland. A tornado kills over 20 people in my original hometown of London, Kentucky (Laurel County).

Boomers are working more years than any other generation, while others have taken early retirement and picked up part-time jobs.

Because Boomers overpopulate everything, ground is broken across America to build more nursing homes, condos, villas anything to house this massive generation.

This may sound odd, but… if your parents owned a funeral home, a hospice facility, or a memorial garden **YOU** are about to come into great wealth.
Boomers are dying so fast in Florida, it's three a month in the Water Oak Community where I live. (Granted, some of those folks were born in the 1930s.)

By 2030, we Boomers born in 1948 will be **82 years old**.
There were nearly 100 students in my graduation class at London High School in Kentucky. Nearly a third are already **dead**. You can apply that same "one-third gone" stat to my EKU class of 1970: 1,000 out of 3,000 are gone. WKU 1973? Same story: 1,000 of the 4,000 who sat on the E.A. Diddle Arena floor… have ended work, parenting, and life.

"Death is a part of living" … and now, Boomers feel that truth.

In my nightly prayers, I thank God for this long life.
But WAIT my Granddaddy Mosley lived to age 94. If that holds true... I've got another 17 years.
Or 17 more years of being old and feeble? I'll pass on 94.

FINAL WILLS, TRUSTS, ESTATE PLANNING...

No wonder so many seniors do a lousy job with "end of life" planning.

True story:
Once, while driving through the countryside, I happened upon a lovely memorial garden just a few miles from home. I *did it my way* (as usual). I pulled into the cemetery near Leesburg and drove around. It was beautiful, very beautiful, like the place where I laid my dear mother to rest near Lexington, Kentucky.

At the front was a small business office. I walked in. They politely asked if I had done any pre-planning.
"Good Lord, no," I exclaimed.

She quickly added, "If you pre-plan, you could cut the costs by more than 50%."
She asked if I was a veteran. Then she walked me to the veteran section of the grounds and said the magic words:

"If you are a veteran, your plot will be free."

Now she had my full attention.

I spent an hour with her, and before I left, I had picked a plot, a head marker, a vault, a casket—and since they worked directly with Page-Theus Funeral Home in Leesburg–Wildwood, that decision was also made. I agreed to pay a little more than $100/month (automated), and within no time, I had paid for **everything**.

You wouldn't believe the relief and satisfaction that day brought me.

Since my daughter was squeamish about this, I made all the plans for her.

Boomers still above ground listen to me:

Make an appointment. Talk about pre-planning with a funeral director. If it feels awkward, go to another town. Ask those difficult questions. They will help you. Shop and compare.

Millions of Boomers have done pre-planning. You can too.

Pick someone in your family who is strong-willed. Not faint of heart. An organizer. A planner. A "take charge" person and share your final wishes. Ask them if they're willing to help.

My sister Connie had four children. One of her daughters **Karen Bentley Cobb** said,

"Sure, Uncle Mike. I'll be glad to help you with all your final plans."

Karen is strong-willed, independent, educated, a planner, and trustworthy. I'm eternally grateful.

A Quick Reminder of Life's Unpredictability:

A man who lived three doors from me was cooking breakfast while his wife was doing her makeup.
Then came the stroke.
"I heard her hit the floor," he told me. She was **dead**.

They were snowbirds from Normal, Illinois. The husband wanted to take her back home.
The funeral director quoted $9,000 for a flight to Chicago.
But the man said, "No thanks. I'll drive her."

And he did. After reviewing state laws, the next day, he put his embalmed wife in a dry ice container in the trunk and drove her himself.

When I told this story to neighbors, they all said:

"Yes, Mike. It's true."

But *if I* had tried this? You know I'd hit a deer near Chattanooga, and the cop would say:

"Mr. Mosley, who's the dead lady in the trunk of your car? Come with us."

Reality Check:

Many neighbors here in Florida have made **no plans**.
A funeral now costs **over $10,000**. Add transport to the

Midwest? That's $15,000+.

85% of Boomers in Florida end up cremated—not by choice, but because of what's left in the bank after 10–12 years of retirement living.

Looking Ahead: 2030 to 2040

We will become the **Fading Generation**. Our modest wealth will be transferred.

What really bothers some Boomers (but *not me*), is that by 2040, America will become a **majority non-white nation**. This drives the racists crazy.

"You won't have a country!" Trump.
What a racist he is. His father too.

Diversity is the spice of life.

But we Boomers still own **$19 trillion in real estate**. After we're gone, Social Security and Medicare won't seem so impossible to fix.

Wealth will be handed down, up, over, and under.
In my case, **Western Kentucky University** will benefit. My scholarship fund is already named: **The Michael D. Mosley Scholarship**, for students in Laurel, Pulaski, Russell, or McCreary County.

But wait, I'm not dead yet.

We Boomers of 1948 have lived through:

- ☒ Presidents from Truman to Trump

- ☒ 2 added states

- ☒ 2 Presidents and 1 Pope shot

- ☒ Queen Elizabeth II's entire reign

- ☒ The Cold War

- ☒ The rise of AI

- ☒ The 747, space exploration, and yes, we were even baptized in the River Jordan

CONCLUSION

I hope this book has gotten Boomers thinking, wondering, planning, praying…
If you've done any of those **my work here is done**.

May you live a long life filled with good food, good neighbors, good health, and good friends.

As a good Methodist, baptized in the River Jordan in 2014, I'm just about ready to go.

And I pray your heart is ready for our Savior, Jesus, who said:

"I go to prepare a place for you… and where I go, ye too shall go."

May the next generation lead with decency, unity, love of country, and deep respect for the Constitution.
Defend it with your life, if need be.

God be with you till we meet again.

—Michael D. Mosley, Author

SOURCES

Peterson, Robin. *Elder Centers of Brevard.* Viera, Florida, 2025.

Day, Abby. *Professor, University of London.* London, 2013.

Jones, A. *Age of Openness.* Pew Research Center, Washington, D.C., 2005.

Williams, Bernard. *Marketing Boomers.* Illinois Periodicals, UNI, 1999.

Parachini, Allan. "The Book of Middle Age." *Los Angeles Times*, Los Angeles, 1986.

Quincy, Laura. *The Center for Retirement Research.* Boston, May 2023.

A & E Global Media. Charlotte and New York City, USA, 2023.

Surz, Ron. *Boomer Votes Sway Election.* Boston, Massachusetts, USA, 2024.

www.ingramcontent.com/pod-product-compliance
Lightning Source LLC
Chambersburg PA
CBHW070955120626
46546CB00004B/1627